Bird in the Hand

poems by

Lianne Spidel

DOS MADRES

2014

DOS MADRES PRESS INC.

P.O.Box 294, Loveland, Ohio 45140

www.dosmadres.com   editor@dosmadres.com

Dos Madres is dedicated to the belief that the small press is essential to the vitality of contemporary literature as a carrier of the new voice, as well as the older, sometimes forgotten voices of the past. And in an ever more virtual world, to the creation of fine books pleasing to the eye and hand.

Dos Madres is named in honor of Vera Murphy and Libbie Hughes, the "Dos Madres" whose contributions have made this press possible.

Dos Madres Press, Inc. is an Ohio Not For Profit Corporation and a 501 (c) (3) qualified public charity. Contributions are tax deductible.

Executive Editor: Robert J. Murphy

Illustration & Book Design: Elizabeth H. Murphy
www.illusionstudios.net

Typset in Adobe Garamond Pro & Bambino
ISBN 978-1-939929-09-9
Library of Congress Control Number: 2014933727

First Edition

ACKNOWLEDGEMENTS

Atlanta Review: "Anna, Three Days Old," "Before There Were
　　　Barbies," "Mrs. Powers and the Powers That Be"
Cloudbank: "November Birthday"
The Comstock Review: "The Sweet Gum Lets Its Colors Fall"
Emrys Journal: "Boy Stories
English Journal: "Summer School"
Evening Street Review: "The Common Stones He Saved"
Everything Stops and Listens, Ohio Poetry Association anthology:
　　　"Before the Rain"
Grand Lake Review: "The Tutor, Blue Creek, Ohio" (as "Splice"),
　　　"Imploding Hudson's"
Hawaii Pacific Review: "Comh Bhrón Dhuith"
Heartlands: "The Woodcarver of Sligo"
Hubbub: "Wintering," "Whereabouts, the Question of Suzanne"
The MacGuffin: "16mm Movie, Detroit, Michigan, 1940" (as "16
　　　mm Movies")
Main Street Rag: "Fixers"
Memoir Journal: "Lea at Ninety-five," "16mm Movie:
　　　Melbourne, Florida, 1938"
Ohio Poetry Day prize book: "In the Gallery"
Poetry: "My Twenty-Eighth Grade Book," "Before the Rain"
　　　"Aromatherapy," "Royalty"
Rattle: "Homeland in an Old War," "Mustachio," "Ambassador
　　　Bridge"
Rockhurst Review: "Aunt Tudy's Kidneys"
Rhino: "Paper Hats"
Runes: "Daughters of Eve"
Shenandoah: "Snowfall at Solstice"
Southern Poetry Review: "Birdcalls"
Thema: "The Renaissance Child," "The Climber"
Wisconsin Review: "Godspeed." Also, *I Have My Own Song for It:*

Modern Poems of Ohio, University of Akron Press, 2002, and "A Way with Words," by Ron Rollins on the Greenville Poets, *Ohio Magazine*: June 2011

These poems appear in the following chapbooks:
Chrome, Finishing Line Press, 2006: "Paper Hats," "The Wood-carver of Sligo," In the Gallery"
Pairings, with artist Ann Loveland, Dos Madres Press, 2012: "Second Sight," "The Common Stones He Saved," "Before There Were Barbies," "Daughters of Eve"

SPECIAL THANKS

to my writing group, The Greenville Poets, for their friendship, inspiration and necessary criticism--Cathryn Essinger, David and Suzanne Garrison, Belinda Rismiller and Myrna Stone,

to workshop friends and teachers who have helped me learn the craft and possibilities of poetry, especially Ed Davis in Yellow Springs, Ohio; Christopher Bursk in Montpelier, Vermont; and Billy Collins in Galway, Ireland,

to Robert and Elizabeth Murphy, publishers at Dos Madres Press, for their artistry and dedication in the preparation of this manuscript,

to my artist friend Ann Loveland, who shares her work with me--work that often accomplishes what words cannot,

to Susan Blackwell Ramsey, whose book, *A Mind Like This,* won the 2011 Prairie Schooner Book Prize in Poetry from the University of Nebraska Press, and to Bucky Ignatius who served as president and occasional guest critic of the Greater Cincinnati Writers' League for the past five years, for their kind words about this book,

and to the true characters from my life, past and present, who people these pages.

Lianne Spidel

Introduction to *Bird in the Hand*

Memory is a bird in the hand, always with us, underlying or overlaying the present moment where we are supposed to live. Decades later I find myself walking a rocky path in a fragrant woods beside a lake, and I am sixteen again.

Now I have become an indoors-woman, and I love rooms--not the way I love people--but as places of respite where memory reminds me of the places where I belonged in this world, where I was truly at home.

I have learned that we own forever any place we love wholeheartedly, no matter who holds the deed and lives there now. Just to think of that place is to return, no need to ask for a key, no need to intrude. That is the business of memory, and memory is the bird in my hand that listens while my stories tell themselves.

Sometimes memory chirps like a bird and tells all.

Once in a while it sings.

TABLE OF CONTENTS

1.

...back to the bridge...

2.

...a woman's waiting I have come to know...

3.

...Call it homage, more or less...

4.

...the past sweeps low behind us, a green valley...

for

Erin Elizabeth, Sarah, Claire, Annie and Sam

and in memory of Lea Urquhart Valleau, 1900-1996

I.

…back to the bridge…..

Before There Were Barbies

Our dolls had little-girl bodies,
even the taller ones supposed to be older
whose legs were longer, only that.

Some of them had real hair and glass eyes
that opened and closed. They wore
white anklets and leatherette Mary Janes.

We were wartime girls whose parents
turned gray and middle-aged in five long years.
We had no bikes, our shoes always hurt,

and our hems were turned down twice
before our mothers cut up our dresses
for doll clothes. Somehow

there was always a doll for a birthday
or Christmas, certain as a ration book
or a terrifying newsreel at a Saturday matinee.

While faraway children starved
and the faraway world blew up and fell apart,
our grandmothers knitted miniature sweaters.

Even now we cannot part
with our childhood dolls, loved so tenderly
within our years of being safe,

their glass eyes that saw nothing,
their perfect little bodies--sturdy, whole,
unassailable.

Ambassador Bridge

Sometimes, when I was her child, we took
the tunnel underneath the river,
or better, from the high arch of the bridge

she pointed out to me two countries.
Either way she stashed a pound of butter
underneath the seat or something small

in Royal Doulton in her girdle, tilting
her chin at the customs man,
calling him "Officer," cheeky as hell.

Now she grows slight within my arms,
asking, "What day is this? Am I
in Florida? When am I going home?"

and to the puzzled salesman at the door,
"No, we don't live here. We're Canadians
down for the winter." It is May.

The grocery money hidden in her pillow slip
or underneath the bed, she plans escape,
packing her suitcase, then forgetting why.

Somehow the tunnel has reclaimed her,
muffling her voice like the whispery echoes
of tires in that deep cylinder

where we dared not sound the horn
for fear collapse would seal us helpless,
drowning in our Hudson.

If I could find our way back to the bridge,
geography and time might then come clear
and she could show me here and there,

then and now, while two flags thud
against the sky, and on the river far below
small boats skip and wobble in the sun.

Homeland in an Old War

Burke's Pharmacy on the corner of Six Mile
Road, magazines up front, jars and boxes
neat on oak shelves. Cartoon faces--
Fatso, Ratso and Japso--

leer from a bright poster beside a sign
with slanting letters: *Loose Lips
Sink Ships.* I ask my mother what is it
I should not say.

We spend our ration coupons
at the Varsity Market, take our collections
there, balls of tin foil,
cooking grease, smashed cans.

Newspapers and magazines go to school
where on Rubber Drive Day,
I sacrifice my own Popeye and Olive Oyl
on a heap of boots and tires.

In the basement a hole has been cut
into the converted oil furnace. Noisy
flames lick at my father's shirtsleeves
as he shovels coal.

He fits blackout paper to the windows.
If enemy planes make it inland,
he says any pattern of light could lead
to the factories.

Beside the kitchen phone my mother
is screaming. My cousin's plane is down
over England. Eighteen, and he is dead.
And the kitchen two years later but still

so long ago, the day we drop the first
atom bomb, my father on his feet,
newspaper in hand as if it might help him
believe what we have done to the world.

16mm Movie: Melbourne, Florida, 1938

My mother walks the beach, the ocean
rolling in behind her, ink-blue under clouds
traveling in the opposite direction.

She's in her thirties, wearing a swim suit
of navy blue wool, its halter top
without support, and though she hated being

what she called big-busted, she must
have felt good wearing it because she moves
nonchalantly, ignoring the lens

as if she couldn't care less that my father
is taking her picture. Her arms swing a little,
her legs are slim and athletic,

but too short, she used to say.
She isn't flirting for once, or smiling, content
to let the film take her in just as she is

on the best of ordinary days in the not-yet-
center of her life, no make-up, hair
pulled back, proud of what she knows he sees

in her, a day when she owns the long beach,
the focused eye of the man behind the camera,
the sky.

16mm Movie: Detroit, Michigan, 1940

Mother flirts in Persian lamb
and feathered hat while Grandmother
gathers each one close in the swivel
of her glance, tall people, straight
as the trees on Prairie Avenue.

On the verge of laughter they chat
beside a Hudson sedan, Aunt Jo
lifting her chin above her fur, the dent
of her dimple catching shadow,
Dad flashing his Gary Cooper smile.

Clear in their faces is innocence
of all that would change.
Soon, a red-haired son would die
in a war, their visits would stretch
farther apart and end

before long years of losing each other,
one by one. After that, others said,
Prairie Avenue was home for a time
to drug dealers, and strange
rites took place in basement rooms

where we'd played ping pong
and watched home movies, windows
covered with blackout paper to keep us
safe from air raids, the only things
we thought could hurt us then.

Where Will They Go When I'm Gone?

Once in a while a young soldier ambles
    along, toeing out a little,
a fine crease in his khakis.
        He sings, "I've got spurs
that jingle jangle jingle."
    He will go off to be a bombardier
and never come back.

Sometimes in a flash, my mother
    is leaning on the back of Joe Manuel's
vegetable truck in the middle
        of Prairie Avenue, laughing
with a neighbor. She turns, smiling,
    and moves toward the house,
a bunch of beets in each hand.

My father rummages in the kitchen junk
    drawer, or my student Lisa takes
her seat in the front row. She rests
        her head against the wall,
holds up her hands to show a friend
    her fingernails, painted navy blue
and gold, glitter on the thumbs.

They're never there an instant longer
    than Lisa's upward glance, clearer
than the backdrops that exist now
        without them--a chalkboard,
a bus station, a tidy lawn, the window
    through which light braided itself
across the back of a man's shirt.

Aunt Tudy's Kidneys

When my fever reached 106, the cold
sweats stopped. I walked on feet
that moved an inch above the floor.
"Impossible," my husband said, shaking
the thermometer down.
       "You'd be dead."

I knew then I had my aunt's kidneys.
She died before I was born,
before sulfa, at twenty-eight,
close to the age I was
when my kidneys declared war on me.

Up to then I thought I was unique--
don't we all?--but Aunt Tudy
was the sister who nursed my father
through the 1918 flu.
      Maybe I'm payback.

Besides the kidneys, the angles
of her French-Canadian face
in my mirror make me wonder how much
of who I thought I was
is Aunt Tudy finishing up.

She wouldn't believe it either--
An American? How very improbable…

Still, I hope I cherish everything
she wanted and for her sake regret
all my regrets, every hour lost
to grief. She had sorrow enough
of her own.
    She'll get no more from me.

Imploding Hudson's

My newly-married mother spent days
wandering downward from the 13th floor
where her friend Sybil worked in the Bureau
of Adjustment, all the way to the second
basement, then home on the streetcar,
her unfulfilled wishes still in her purse.

Later, she dragged me there by the arm,
jaywalking across Woodward,
a man with a megaphone scolding us
from a high window. Once inside
we straightened our skirts
and our spines for lunch in the tearoom,

consommé in a silver bowl for me,
and a Mickey Mouse sundae. The first
summer I was old enough, I worked
in bathing suits, cutting off the tags
for women who wore them home, duty-free
under their clothes to Windsor.

My Nancy Drews came from there,
my first bra, everyone's bridal silver--
each bride watching at her window
for the familiar green truck--
my first child's shirts and sleepers,
seconds from the basement, 50¢.

Before they took it down, it had waited
for years, as many of us do,
for things to go right again,
and after all, there was nothing
left inside except the walnut paneling
and the dreams of three generations.

Aromatherapy

The crafty shop, claustrophobic
with its hooked rugs and sweatered
teddy bears, its pungent potpourri
of rose or watermelon, sends me flying

as I did long ago from my mother's
fox fur collar, the pointed noses
under stony eyes nudging
my cheeks, wafting Arpège.

I do my best to empathize
with my friend Ginny who,
when her dog died,
longed for puppy breath,

but for me, nostalgia is good
Canadian air blowing across a driveway
in Detroit, ozone after lightning,
a peeled orange.

Elegant men's stores up their sales
by piping in a subliminal scent
called "line-dried linen."
More power to them

and to those who treat subway patrons
to the smell of chocolate chip
cookies baking, causing them
to shove each other less.

I'm grateful I can no longer catch
a whiff of my grade school cafeteria
with its scalded metal trays, hot
dogs, canned peas, waxy milk cartons

but still savor an odoriferous moment
in the old Neisner's on Six Mile Road
where I stood listening
to Fats Domino find his thrill,

where inklings of romance mingled
in a bouquet with roasted peanuts
and cheap chocolate, mothballs,
oilcloth and Old Dutch.

Mrs. Powers and the Powers That Be

*Ensō is the Japanese word for circle, also a sacred symbol
in the Zen school of Buddhism....Only a person mentally
and spiritually complete can draw a true ensō.*

When the bell rang, we took our seats
as she stood before us, all four feet seven
of her, including the white topknot
of her hair. Silence ruled as her eyes
slid over ours to assure herself
that every one of us was watching

before she faced the board and raised
a clean stem of chalk in her right hand.
She positioned the chalk and, with one
dramatic forward motion, completed
a perfect circle in one fell swoop,
the point of its connection indiscernible.

My terror of all things mathematical forgotten,
I opened my pencil box, breathed its sweet
wooden smell and swung the free leg
of my compass to create my own circle
in my notebook, the disc of a tiny world,
its pinpoint center equidistant from every arc.

If the brilliant and terrible Andrew twins
had traded classes that day, as they frequently
did, Mrs. Powers refused to notice. No class
ever conspired to drag her to the closet
and lock her in as legend insisted
had happened to a less revered teacher.

I thought of her yesterday, the first time
I ever heard of an ensō, remembering how
I conquered the two-dimensional world
with well-sharpened pencils and the sunrise
curve of my protractor, how everything
came out even and stayed that way all day.

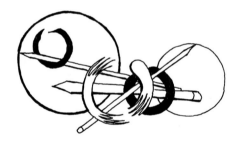

2.

...a woman's waiting I have come to know......

Daughters of Eve

I have found DNA in skeletons thousands of years
old and seen exactly the same genes in my own friends...
we are all connected through our mothers to only
a handful of women living tens of thousands of years ago.
--Bryan Sykes,
The Seven Daughters of Eve, 2001

If my mother had an inkling of the mystery
of dividing cells, I'm sure she never thought
of them as I do, a line of ragtag recruits
committed to making a new person.

I'd like to tell her that she passed to me one
constant strain, tidy as spices lined
on her kitchen shelf: cinnamon, nutmeg,
cloves, those her mother used, and hers before,

that the clan mothers were hunters who bore
their daughters in caves, that perhaps
the one the scientist called Tara claims us,
Tara, who never saw the green-hilled land

my mother's mother never saw, who may
have played a flute made from the wing bone
of a swan and strung a dozen strands of shells,
may have worn them to her sand dune grave.

I would say, Mother, of all who came before,
no one knows whose laugh you made your own,
whose stubbornness, but one of seven laid
down in you good tinder for a necessary fire.

You used to say you wondered how you got me
anyway, always my father's child.
Know how you gave me the flame of my self
that ends with me, a mother of sons.

Before the Rain

Minutes before the rain begins
I always waken, listening
to the world hold its breath,
as if a phone had rung once in a far
room or a door had creaked
in the darkness.

Perhaps the genes of some forebear
startle in me, some tribal warrior
keeping watch on a crag beside a loch,
miserable in the cold,

though I think it is a woman's waiting
I have come to know,
a Loyalist hiding in the woods,
muffling the coughing of her child
against her linen skirts, her dark head
bent over his, her fear spent
somewhere else in time,

leaving only this waiting,

and I hope she escaped
with her child, and I suppose she did.
If not, I wouldn't be lying here awake,
alive, listening for the rain to begin
so that she can run, the sound
of her footsteps lost, the sight
of them blotted away on the path.

Godspeed

--for John and Annie Glenn

During his first orbit, I lay
in a hospital bed, wrapped
in a piano concerto by Brahms
which someone had turned on
by accident, my black-haired son
bundled in his cart, caught up
in the first of wordless dreams
he would never learn to compromise,
while an Ohio-born traveler
circled our adventure with his own.

When we met him years later,
stumping Ohio in the seventies,
he crinkled his eyes and said
I looked like Annie. She told me
they ate by candlelight every night,
even if it was only hot dogs.

Last week my son, late bloomer,
weightless with euphoria, married
the girl he said he had to have,
and today the old astronaut,
launched safely again into space,
comments on the beauty of Hawaii,
where perhaps the honeymooners
find a moment to shield their eyes
and scan the sky.

On my refrigerator, a clipping--
Annie brave in a pale hat,
her balding husband's hand
on her shoulder, reminder
that all adventurers who soar
must then descend, survive
the terrors of re-entry, and find
their footing on this common ground.

The Climber

As a toddler, he once tumbled
the length of a staircase.
The imprinted tread on his forehead
lasted a day, branded me forever.

A few years later, he slid down
into the gears of a steam thresher
parked in the alley, pinned in so close
I couldn't lift him out.

A neighbor, a wrestler in his youth,
plunged bulging arms down
to extract him, held him dangling
for a moment like a fish.

He climbed the TV tower behind our house,
surveyed fenced yards, treetops,
the town beyond. Far below in the yard,
I made my voice easy,

"Time to come down, Johnny, right now,"
which he did, one shoelace hanging,
ribs jutting under his tee-shirt
with each even breath.

Still dazed with height, he saw
my fear, my need to gather him in
and smother even that last brightness
he'd saved. Intact to the dimple

in his right cheek, the dirt
under his fingernails, he clenched
his hands around the memory
of metal poles and a place in the sky.

The Common Stones He Saved

Home from the hunt at suppertime,
      he would open his hand, each line
etched in sweaty grime, to reveal a point
          unearthed by the plow, tip
intact, the color of sand or sunset
      or obsidian.

He wondered, he said later, who
      had touched it last, before it felled
an animal or was lost in the ransacking
         of a village, then the stab
of epiphany as he measured the time--
      2000 years--against his own eleven.

In winter he turned to the common stones
      he'd saved, plugged in the rock tumbler,
exchanging rougher grit for finer,
         washing between, loving the feel
of polish over form, the first sight
      of true color.

Then spring again, the hunt for fossils
      disgorged in the rush of creeks:
cephalopod, horn coral, the rare
         trilobite, little triune god,
its symmetry of bound segments
      unmarred by 400 million years.

He was nearly grown
  when we left behind the hills
of limestone and shale, oceanless tides
    deep and still within them.
After that, the stones he found
      were only common ones.

The House on Logan's Lane

The neighbor children told ours
that someone had died in the house,
asked who had to sleep in that bedroom
and if any of us had seen the ghost.

Someone had painted the room the purple
of iris, then walked the paint
across the floor. We papered over a tropical
seascape on the living room wall.

All spring the boys ran down the green
spine of ridge into the woods, their dog
close behind--the one later banished
for raiding the neighbor's chickens,

and sometime after the summer wind blew
through windows too high to see out, our lives
fell into place. We put away our socks
in the drawers as if we would forever.

Later, when nails in the driveway
flattened twelve tires, when the phone rang
at midnight with farewell messages, even then
the house seemed more haven than prison.

Driving away, we hung a grapevine wreath
on the back of the moving van, watched
the bravado of flapping ribbons, wisps
of baby's breath escaping in the wind.

We left a tangle of bikes and outgrown games,
purple footprints carpeted over, a ghost
or two, and sealed beneath sedate stripes,
wild whitecaps and a brazen sea.

The Tutor, Blue Creek, Ohio

The counselor brought to her a first grader
from the hollow who wouldn't speak, small
for her age, eyes unreadable, fair hair
smelling of wood smoke.

In the bathroom the tutor showed her
how to flush, how not to be afraid
of the noise, of the rush of water
like the creek at flood time.

Afternoons when they read, the child's dark
eyes sank into the books, her careful fingers
moved to the corners of the pages to turn them.
Watching her, the tutor recalled

a time-lapse film in botany class
where petals of a blossom had sprung open,
overturned as in the church-and-steeple game,
then folded inward to twist again into bud.

She saw how, long before she spoke,
the child collected words and gestures,
took them into herself like a spent blossom
impossibly retrieving its petals.

Now in spring the tutor thinks of her,
imagines her emerging, long-legged now,
from hovel into hollow, her hair washed clean,
with redbud and dogwood unfurling.

My Twenty-Eighth Grade Book

stows seven pages in alphabetical order,
last names first, Joshes and Jaimes, Brians
and Mikes. Over these years I've learned
I can always count on girls named Stephanie,
believe I could have found a better name

for any Brandi, Brie or Angel. I like
to say aloud names that end with *a*--
Melissa, Marisa, Terra, Aaliyah--
and the simple boys' names that hang
on the air like flags--Bob, Tom, Joe.

Amy Templeton's name clings cloudlike,
and Aaron Guthrie's looks so pithy on the page
it seems a guarantee that someday he will run
a bank, while the syllables for Dominique
Jones swing-step and halt with a bow.

My years of careful lettering
will end before the Jakes arrive in quantity
with the girls called Kelsie and Taylor.
I didn't think I could forget
a single Paul, Steve, Jon or any one

of the great decade of Matthews, yet now
they meld together in memory, huge-footed,
limber-limbed, easy beside the pale slivers
of girls who dreamed into their spiral
notebooks, less defined in my mind than those

whose names, long ago, shared a grade book
with my own and whose faces are separate
still, sweet as ever with their brush cuts
and saddle shoes: Janet, Margaret, Larry,
Seymour, Joyce, Roger, Nancy, Ann.

Summer School

Because I needed to know for a poem,
I asked the science teacher sitting
next to me (the one they teased
about his massive chest) to explain
to me the composition of a cloud.

He had already told me he was there
only for the credit, a step up
on the salary scale. His wife
wanted a bigger house, the kids
were growing, he was overwhelmed

with bills and coaching.
I said, "When you're my age
it will empty out.
There's too much, then all
at once there's almost nothing."

When he answered me about the cloud,
his voice went soft:
"Moisture on dust," and when
I asked him "in" or "on,"
he said it didn't matter

either way. We never shared
a coffee and spoke only
of casual things, a still viable
jock and a graying grandmother
pretending to concentrate on the course

content, side by side through indolent
hours, easy in the peaceful co-
existence a couple of prepositions
had provided--a gentle affinity,
pleasure like moisture on dust.

Boy Stories

*The owl said, "Hoo! Hoo! You were a bad
little bear to run away from home."*
          --from A Little White Teddy Bear
            by Dorothy Sherrill

My sons leaned closer
to see the picture of a small bear
lost in the snow with only
                    his galoshes and red cap.

At bedtime in their Sears pajamas,
afternoons when they were rank
with sweat and grass,
I read to them about the baby shark
with phenomenal hearing
or the contemplative bull
who loved to think
                    under a cork tree.

Decades later they tell me
their stories, adventures involving
water towers and forbidden
tunnels, an icy night on I-70
when their car spun four
full turns under an overpass
and an evening when one of them
                    downed eighteen Little Kings.

I say, "You survived. I don't
want to listen any more,"
but having warmed to their subject,
they will not stop telling.

Second Sight

--for Dr. Jeffrey Horwitz

1.
Orderlies in ghostly greens share
jokes, lean against the gurney
urging on the one whose job it is
to cut off my eyelashes.
                              Trained
in tranquility, they circle close
to tie my wrists to the rails.

My retinas are screens.
The doctor will laser every hole,
band the right eye--too far gone--
with nylon. I trust
                        his small hands,
the choice he's made to work at night
                        when the world wears rubber soles.

2.
When morning light sifts through
the bandages, I pry up an edge
to see a wall gone sallow in shadow
next to one dazzled gold
                              by sun,
the clean vertical between them,
a television set, blue December sky.

3.
Weeks later, faced with a display
of paisley ties that dare me to focus--
colors and patterns whirling
as I blink,
                I buy four, dizzy
in love with them, then stumble
out into sunlight,
bumping into everything, admiring
the grey curb with its yellow rim,
buildings meeting pavement dead on,
the figure
                on the corner,
her sturdy shoes and prim cape,
her kettle filling with coins.

To My Ex-Husband, Thank You for Your Gift of a Hot Tub Membership

The Christmas you left, you sent me
a nightgown from a catalog, cotton
threaded with wool and a Peter Pan collar--
not the lingerie I'd wished for.
You knew how cold I'd be.

The next year a winter coat arrived,
mauve, color of bruises, with a hood
to hide in. Its quilted fiberfill
served as gentle armor,
kept my own heat safe inside.

Now that winter melts to spring
outside a steamed glass door,
an add-on to my Y card
grants me entry to a blue-tiled room.
There I sink into tumbling water

where heaps of foam bank
and bobble, where hot-fingered jets
pink my skin and pulse
across my lower back--not your fire,
not mine--but warm is warm.

Fixers

I never fail to check out men
        who wander the aisles
of my favorite hardware store,
            pausing in comfortable shoes
before bins of hinges, jingling
       the coins in their pockets.

Familiar with fuses and circuit
        breakers, intimate
with a plumb line, they know
          wood screws from metal,
own tin snips, drill bits
      and a miter box.

Whether CPA's, farmers, Sunday
       golfers or those who work
second shift, when faced
         with furnace filters,
pilot lights or primer,
     they think alike.

Whatever their level of skill,
       they aim to please with coping
saw or caulking gun,
         sensitive to the ins
and outs of a power tool
     or a dimmer switch.

One of them, waiting beside me
     in line, eyes my malfunctioning
sweeper as if he'd like
         to jump right in and fix it
on the spot--or take a stab
     at it. I pretend

not to notice, admire him
     as he fidgets. Who can resist
a man on a mission to make
         something work just
right, one who whistles softly
     while he ponders how?

Mustachio

Six a.m. in the Y pool, the swimmer
in the next lane flashes me a grin
before flipping into his turn,
and I ask myself why I never liked
a mustache on a man.

It might have been those childhood
newsreels--a face with mad eyes
and a censor's black mark riding
the lip--but the swimmer's has charm,
stays tidy even when wet.

Uncle Marcel curled his into sheep
horns, polished his bald pate, clues
to his jaunty mood, foreshadowings of fun--
and it does take a certain frame
of mind to grow one:

Picture a man at the bathroom mirror
contemplating the planes of his face,
asking himself if there's room, if
it will be the right color or make
his chin recede,

imagining a suave accoutrement to a well-
cut suit, a comfortable accessory
to chinos and an open-necked shirt
or, from memory, Errol Flynn bravado
and a red neckerchief.

Even the dash of the word sells itself--
moustache, something a man can do
that a woman can't, at least
not happily--an asset, an extra eyebrow
quirked above a smile.

Paper Hats

--for Gerald Stern

I thought of you today, Gerald Stern,
while I made paper hats
with my granddaughters, a project
involving scissors and small sponges
for painting, as well, of course,
as paper, which you said
Galileo compared to the mind.

There was no time for poems, for a walk
to Bickford's to sip tea. Glitter
glue sparkled on the carpet and noses
needed wiping. The little one,
who loves nakedness, had to be coaxed
again into her shirt and overalls,
to cover her shoulder blades,
which reminded me all morning
of the nubs of wings.

I remembered the squirrel in your poem,
the one you preferred to the paper
mind, because of the children
who ran through this house today,
beautiful and wild, and fell asleep
on the floor, their fair hair
with its darker winter streaks
flung back from their foreheads.
Tonight they pose for their parents
in paper hats tied with leftover
ribbons, and we clap and cheer.

Do I seem to be going on and on?
No offense, but you do that too at times,
and there are other things you said
that I'm sure I understand, like the pity
you feel for poets in this life,
and your sympathy for Zane Grey,
who gave himself to his passion
for the desert even though
his diction didn't match his dreams,

and most of all how you want
to stamp yourself into the sand,
become a giant angel *with footprints
like a bear's*, and you want him huge,
and you want a child or two
to notice and to see you fly.

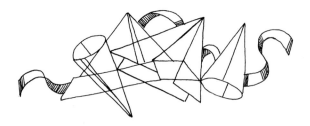

3.

...Call it homage, more or less......

River Song for the Grandmother I Never Knew

Full of salmon and the music of mad fiddles,
the Corrib River churns, rushing the tide,
defying the margins of its banks
with wild rhythms of forgotten songs.

The Corrib River churns, rushing the tide.
When it leaps to crescendo
with wild rhythms of forgotten songs,
echoes of dancing feet ring along the waves.

When it leaps to crescendo,
fiddles crowd and clash, racing over stones.
Echoes of dancing feet ring along the waves,
beating out loss and sorrow, fury and joy.

Fiddles crowd and clash, racing over stones.
My grandmother's feet come flying,
beating out loss and sorrow, fury and joy
as I call out to travel with her now.

My grandmother's feet come flying.
She leaps into place among the dancers
as I call out to travel with her now--
Grandmother, find me, leave no stone unturned.

She leaps into place among the dancers
in this magical river dizzy with sun.
Grandmother, find me, leave no stone unturned.
Grab me by an ankle, pull me by my hair.

In this magical river dizzy with sun,
we become the river, we become the dance.
Grab me by an ankle. Pull me by my hair.
Together we'll chase down everyone we've lost.

Garden Wedding with Ohio Fight Song

The music livens after the bride dances
with her father on a wooden floor set
in the garden. Four women move together
then, laughing at the song which draws them.

Pink, blue, ivory dresses merge, and the lace
bodice of the gown the bride's mother wears
almost covers her scars. Their arms, tanned
in summer gardens, reach for each other

and connect. Their heads pull close--pale
gold and burnished, cropped red, a Nefertiti
triangle (a silver shimmer fanning wide
where once not long ago no hair grew.)

Inside their circle rest their sharings--flowers
and babies tended, marriages challenged,
parents lost to death, hard words spoken
aloud--spina bifida, bone marrow transplant.

No one has taught them the steps.
They know this dance as well
as they know the seasons or the unmarked
trail between terror and triumph.

Their arms rest easy
on each other's shoulders as they circle,
singing in evening's waning light,
"Sloopy, Hang On."

Comh Bhrón Dhuith

in memory of Collette Eikenberry

On your last day you lay
lily-white in the big brass bed,
old scars criss-crossing your breast,

Your hair not long enough to muss,
your body cold to touch,
though you said hot, kicked off

the coverlet, lay spare and elegant
without it, while each breath
came in two pieces.

Outside the maples, restless,
tossing, everyone again and again
watering your impatiens heaped

by the doorsill. Inside, quietly,
the table to be set, the food
prepared, the counter scrubbed.

Afterward, they laid you out in white,
lined your eyes, placed snapshots
underneath your fingers, each nail

painted clear, left you on an October
hillock, a tree above you swaying,
shedding, cows in a near field lowing.

I wanted them to bury you upright
in a sandpit like a Celtic queen,
spear in hand, facing the enemy

wearing your good gold rings, a cross
set with jewels on your mutilated
breast, your hair still growing,

displacing sand tendril by tendril,
red flames spilling the heat
of your living at the core of the earth.

Whereabouts...the Question of Suzanne

The harshest winter finds in us an invincible summer.
--Albert Camus

The world must be to you an alien planet now,
its familiarity an affront to her leaving,
taken from you in the month of Christmas,
the holiday displaced by parody,

a caricature of joy in a wretched winter
when trees twisted black branches
into graceless snarls
as if they had forgotten what leaves are,

and the wind bit like an angry dog, whipped
at your ankles, whined in your ears.
At least you knew the fury of the cold
could not touch her. Even in her pain,

her gentle voice eased yours, her human love
attending to your own, making light
of suffering. "How ridiculous this is,"
she'd say to you, seeing your despair,

and now, her presence beside you
so strong, except, you said, you could no longer
touch her skin. She was a person of faith,
and with the geography of heaven

a mystery, where is she in our reality,
in terms perhaps of light years, real--
yet not confined by our place and time,
the *where* and *when* fastening us to earth?

Did you notice, with a new month,
the morning when the landscape changed
after a night of frozen fog, waking
to the trees rimed with ice like feathers,

pillared soft against the sky, a forest
of poplar clouds pinned to earth and lifted
like gloved hands? I thought of her and then
of you, and when the rime melted away,

the bare branches had softened from black to brown
and held themselves aloft under the blue charity
of sky, buoyant in the cold as if, after all
they remembered sunlight and leaves.

--for Richard Veler

Anna, Three Days Old

The gentle Lab sniffs
at her intricate ear, while somewhere
among far-away footsteps
her sister sings. Anna sleeps
frog-legged, her porcupine hair
                    quilling the sheet.

All night long the rain has fallen,
sheathing this house on the hill,
soaking the sugar maple, weighing down
its branches to swaddle the trunk.
Slim fingers gathered in, Anna sleeps
                    in a rose-walled room.

The school bus pauses, motor
humming at the foot of the driveway
where rivulets of water still run.
When Anna stirs, her mother
will feed her and swab the stub
                    of cord that clings,

remnant of a chamber hung with wavering
filaments, where a sprout pouch
nested, where a cluster of genes
burrowed deep, and blood vessels fine
as hairs etched her skin
                    in a full-body tattoo,

a domain of somersault and free swim,
a cave that held her in an orange
glow when her mother stood in sunlight
and sent her downward finally,
full of her secrets, to the world
                    which enslaves her now

with air and hunger, which will enchant her,
which may sadden and betray her,
which this morning
on the grass beneath her window
lays down a crimson welcome for her,
                    leaf by leaf.

Royalty

"I gave birth to a princess," her mother
once told me, and I thought of my son pouring
his grape-nuts in the garage so as not to wake her,

of the moment her baby, seeing her
now a separate entity, seemed not to breathe,
refused to blink her sapphire eyes.

I remembered again last night as she
and I crossed a Florida street, the caution
light running gold streamers

over the dark sweep of her hair,
when a young man coming toward us halted
midway a moment, stunned, before moving on.

So what is this Divine Right--less
than bloodlines, or more? More than symmetry
of face or a silver necklace nestled

at a flawless throat, the nerve to send back
bad food in restaurants, more than the big,
loopy handwriting of the generous spirit?

Call it bravery, that eager readiness
in the eyes, the quality of the light shining
there. Call it blessed assurance.

Today, pony-tailed, she luxuriates in sun,
opulent in a hot pink bikini. In deference
the ocean leans away, a backdrop.

I find myself bent, studying the shore for perfect
shells to lay at her feet--cat's paw, prickly
cockle, angel wing. Call it homage, more or less.

The Woodcarver of Sligo

Over and over, into the folds
of Ceithlinn's skirts, Micheal peels
the triple spirals signifying
breasts and womb, interspersed
with crude fish and animals.

Ceithlinn emerges from his hands
riding the back of Andagna Mór,
her husband, as the carver marks
their peasant faces, their sturdy
merged forms. He tells their story

to a knot of tourists as his chisel
bites the sycamore, his arms moving
white and smooth beneath rolled
sleeves, sinews and veins polished
by afternoon light at the window,

he himself a bending statue edged
by sunlight, just as this morning
beyond the bus window, the mountain
Knocknarea posed and poses still--
a reclining nude whose distant curve

leans blue and green from hip
to flattened breast. There the circle
of a rocky cairn rises,
some say, at the burial place
of Maeve, the ancient queen.

The woman-mountain dreams on, ever
at the moment of awakening,
nipple of cairn pressing toward clouds,
roughened forever by the touch
of some forsaken god.

Birdcalls
--for Sam, three months old

When the crow calls, *caw, caw,*
you study the sky
from your stroller, and when
I mimic the cry,

you smile and look beyond me,
waiting for the true *caw,*
caw, with its answer
farther off.

Here also can be heard
the twitter of gentler birds
on a morning when sound itself
is everything

but it is the *caw* you crave,
its rigidity in autumn air,
the perfect arc
of its diminuendo.

Your eyes search the trees,
source of a voice once heard
you'll never remember
not knowing

that splits the sky the sky with two
rousing syllables not meant
for you but calling to you
all the same.

4.

...The past lies low behind us, a green valley...

The Sweet Gum Lets Its Colors Fall

Autumn leaves make lonely work, a waste
of time spent on waste in a season
of war when the news is death in desert
dust and filth, stench and offal,
awful death.

I'd welcome Frost's tramps--you know,
the two he hired in mud time to do his chores,
the chores he said he'd rather do himself.
I half believe him, but wish for naïve boys
with rakes from another generation,

for childhood evenings when fathers
gathered to burn the leaves in piles
along the street while we waited
in our school shoes to stamp the ashes
and went to sleep smelling smoke in our hair.

Now in misty drizzle the last tree is dropping
fast, the sweet gum in my neighbor's yard,
sending its leaves skipping toward me
one by one--gold, bronze, cordovan
and aubergine--every one a goner

like this yellow one with crimson spots
along its veins, but what a way to go--
afloat, guided by the slim rudder of a stem
to spread-eagle shining on the grass
before my rake. I am shamed

by world-weariness, by my human body,
by the grace and silence of the gum tree,
its leaves in their leave-taking
nothing like young men and women
sent to die in uproar and terror.

Stripped and chill,
the gum tree has given up its beauty
in a glory dance of death,
wearing just its burrs now, prayer beads
clustered in the rain.

Wintering

The winter of your father's last
illness we sped to him on icy roads
scooped from walled snow, flying
through one-way tunnels to heaven.

It's like that now. I clear
the walk from my front door in a swath
exactly as wide as my shovel,
and every day the small banks rise.

Sometimes the past returns
in a few white stitches in the night
sky, amounting to nothing,
sometimes in a blizzard,
irresponsible, out of control.

Sometimes, like now, it adds
to itself each night, little
by little, until finally
a coverlet of what has been
obliterates the world.

Even the present numbs
in the face of this landscape,
when a moment of regret startles
us, a slick of black ice
to bring us to our knees.

In the Gallery

--for G.J.S

Once you would have walked with me
here where silent patrons
circle bronzes by Degas:
Dancer Putting on Her Stocking,
Woman in a Tub, Horse Preparing
To Leave the Ground.

The brochure says the artist
was like you--sarcastic, melancholy,
but none of that means anything today
when action frozen in time is all
that matters, when it is clear to me
that I miss you most in motion:

your quick step up at the kitchen
door or slow meander down holiday
streets, adventure lifting
your heels. When the earphones
tell me that the artist's choice
of awkward moments gives the work

tension and energy, I see
the backward thrust of your neck
before laughter. Where a horse
lifts a twist of wire for a hoof,
I learn how sometimes the wax
melted away when the pieces

were cast, how they suffered
in transition, and in that I find
myself, not you, here where
your gestures stun me
with their absence, where no one
has known to save them in bronze.

Lea at Ninety-Five

At fifteen, freed from school
and the farm she hated,
she washed the colored clothes
for a family of seven to pay her keep,
found work in a bookstore, bought white
boots and a feather boa, fell in love
with a boy thought far above her.

When his father said they were too
young, she raised her chin,
went dancing every night, snared
and scorned three fiancés in turn.
When one turned stubborn,
she threw his ice skates clattering
after him to make herself clear.

At twenty-three she knew she could get
anything with her larkspur eyes
and bookstore education.
She won back her love, escaped Ontario,
kept a house with peach walls and open
windows. Her only child came
as a surprise she made the best of.

She never forget a blizzard one childhood
Christmas Eve, being sledded away
to safety with her sister and brothers
as their older sister strangled
with diphtheria. Her father lived
afterward in a black Scottish mood,
refused to keep Christmas again.

Today all this comes back to her
as I polish her nails and feed her
with a slow spoon. Yet she has no
idea where her man has gone,
and the child she never wanted
has become the sister she never
liked, the one who didn't die.

Bedtime

Barefoot in a nightgown grown too short,
she folds the bedspread down
and turns to the chair to rearrange

the fuzzy dog with its illogical eyelashes
and the red-scarfed Christmas bear,
tucking them closer until their heads touch.

She climbs into bed and pulls the covers
to her chin, puts up her arms for my embrace.
For a moment my gray hair mingles

with hers, pale silk on the pillow.
I switch off the light. "Goodnight,"
she says. I answer, "Goodnight, Mama."

Snowfall at Solstice

I wonder if this might be the night
when you decide to go, with snow
stippling the screen of your small window
and you snug in your chair, wound
in an afghan, full of shepherd's
pie and the sugar cookie dunked for you

in tea. You are at peace. Listening, you
feel the soundless weight of this night,
starless, without sentinel or shepherd,
as heaven comes down to earth in snow
to level each crevice, seal each wound,
fill the cup of space outside your window.

The courtyard framed in the window
is all that remains of the world you
knew, a place where whiteness has wound
the tree with garlands heavy as night,
where there is no respite from snow,
no landmark to be seen by shepherds.

In young years, friends--winter shepherds
and maids--summoned you from any window
when the sky threw itself blue over snow,
over the ice of the Rideau. With them, you
learned ski trails curving into night
up the Gatineau, and every path wound

its way through some adventure, wound
magically toward one who would shepherd
you through cities on starless nights,
whose homecoming you awaited at windows,
who carried your furred boots for you
through seventy winters of snow.

He will find his way in winging snow,
white-haired, a woolen scarf wound
at his neck, coming from darkness to you
stooped but sure-footed as a shepherd,
an overcoated angel reflected in the window,
stamping from his shoes the snow, the night.

When you choose, take the shepherd's arm, leave
the narrow window, walk safe with him by night
out where all stars are wound in snow.

November Birthday

Before the weather turned, I'd meet you
on the shabby deck of a nearby college pub.
Passers-by might have thought
we'd sat here once a week for fifty years
or so, reminiscing over beer and fries--
no idea how new we are at this.

When you come to my place, you bring
coffee beans and pepper bacon,
occasionally lingerie,
and when I visit you, you try to make
your dachshunds like me better,
not to tremble at my unfamiliar touch.

You said once that maybe
we are old enough that nothing bad
will happen to us anymore,
and tonight at my house, we celebrate
by candlelight with Merlot
and strawberries

and my gift of wine glasses
for your new condo. I bought them
for the turning of their split stems,
like the two of us bending
to find the place where we connect
and hold together stronger

than alone, as the past sweeps low
behind us, a green valley
where our lovely ghosts wander
content, while at this table
wine warms our throats
and two small flames defy the dark.

NOTES:

p. 2. "Ambassador Bridge"
The suspension bridge, completed in 1929, connects Detroit, Michigan, with Windsor, Ontario. The bridge and the Detroit-Windsor tunnel make up the busiest international border crossing in America.

p. 10. "Imploding Hudson's"
The J.L. Hudson Company in downtown Detroit was destroyed on October 24, 1998. Built in 1910, the store had 25 floors and employed up to 10,000 workers at a time. It closed in 1983. (Source: Tracy Ward from Michael Hauser, guest curator, "Remembering Downtown Hudson's" at the Detroit Historical Museum.)

p. 17. "Daughters of Eve"
Along with the work of thousands of other modern research scientists, the work of Bryan Sykes (*The Seven Daughters of Eve*, W.W. Norton and Company, 2001) has added to knowledge of the genetic history of *Homo Sapiens*. Reaching his premise with a study of DNA samples, Sykes traced "virtually all 650 million modern Europeans" to seven clan mothers born between 10,000 and 45,000 years ago.

p. 19. "Godspeed"
In addition to its dedication to astronaut John Glenn and his wife Annie, this poem was written to honor the wedding of the poet's son and daughter-in-law, Sara and John, married in 1998.

p. 22. "The Common Stones He Saved"
The local is Adams County, Ohio, a family home from 1973-1981.

p. 37. "Paper Hats"
Lines quoted from Gerald Stern's poems are from *Leaving Another Kingdom* (Harper-Perennial): "The Angel Poem," "At Bickford's," "I Remember Galileo," and "A Hundred Years from Now."

p. 41 "River Song for the Grandmother I Never Knew"
The Corrib River, an estuary running into Galway Bay from the Atlantic, is subject to it tides. The poet's maternal Irish-Canadian grandmother, known for her spirited love of life, people and music, never visited Ireland, and her maiden name and Irish family history remain unknown.

p. 43. "Comh Bhrón Dhuith"
The title, a common phrase on Irish gravestones, is translated from the Gaelic as "Rest in Peace" or "In Memoriam." (Source: an Irish tour bus driver.)

ABOUT THE AUTHOR

LIANNE SPIDEL grew up in Detroit, daughter of an automotive artist to whom her chapbook of art poems, *Chrome*, is dedicated. A retired high school English teacher, she is a graduate of Wittenberg University and of the University of Michigan Rackham School. Her other books are *Pairings*, a chapbook of art and poetry with Michigan artist Ann Loveland, and *What to Tell Joseme*, for which she was named Ohio Poet of the Year, 2013.

ABOUT THE ARTIST

The cover painting, *Gladioli*, and inside art are by Ann Loveland, Michigan Water Color Society and National Watercolor Society member. Her work has been displayed widely both locally and nationally. *Gladioli* was a gold-ribbon winner at the annual Birmingham, Michigan, art show, "Our Town," in 2012.

Books by Dos Madres Press

Richard Luftig - *Off The Map* (2006)

Austin MacRae - *The Organ Builder* (2012)

Mario Markus - *Chemical Poems-One For Each Element* (2013)

J. Morris - *The Musician, Approaching Sleep* (2006)

Rick Mullin - *Soutine* (2012), *Coelacanth* (2013)

Robert Murphy - *Not For You Alone* (2004), *Life in the Ordovician* (2007),
    From Behind The Blind (2013)

Pam O'Brien - *The Answer To Each Is The Same* (2012)

Peter O'Leary - *A Mystical Theology of the Limbic Fissure* (2005)

Bea Opengart - *In The Land* (2011)

David A. Petreman - *Candlelight in Quintero - bilingual edition* (2011)

Paul Pines - *Reflections in a Smoking Mirror* (2011), *New Orleans Variations
    & Paris Ouroboros* (2013)

David Schloss - *Behind the Eyes* (2005)

William Schickel - *What A Woman* (2007)

Lianne Spidel & Anne Loveland - *Pairings* (2012)

Murray Shugars - *Songs My Mother Never Taught Me* (2011),
    Snakebit Kudzu (2013)

Jason Shulman - *What does reward bring you but to bind you to Heaven
    like a slave? (2013)*

Olivia Stiffler - *Otherwise, we are safe* (2013)

Carole Stone - *Hurt, the Shadow- the Josephine Hopper poems* (2013)

Nathan Swartzendruber - *Opaque Projectionist* (2009)

Jean Syed - *Sonnets* (2009)

Madeline Tiger - *The Atheist's Prayer* (2010), *From the Viewing Stand* (2011)

James Tolan - *Red Walls* (2011)

Brian Volck - *Flesh Becomes Word* (2013)

Henry Weinfield - *The Tears of the Muses* (2005),
    Without Mythologies (2008), *A Wandering Aramaean* (2012)

Donald Wellman - *A North Atlantic Wall* (2010),
    The Cranberry Island Series (2012)

Anne Whitehouse - *The Refrain* (2012)

Martin Willetts Jr. - *Secrets No One Must Talk About* (2011)

Tyrone Williams - *Futures, Elections* (2004), *Adventures of Pi* (2011)

Kip Zegers - *The Poet of Schools* (2013)

www.dosmadres.com